FROM
GOD,
TO
MOM,
TO
ME
A MEMOIR

O-haji Moncrief

authorHOUSE®

AuthorHouse™
1663 Liberty Drive
Bloomington, IN 47403
www.authorhouse.com
Phone: 1 (800) 839-8640

Published by AuthorHouse 12/05/2019

ISBN: 978-1-7283-3806-4 (sc)
ISBN: 978-1-7283-3805-7 (e)

Library of Congress Control Number: 2019919339

Print information available on the last page.

Dedication

❋

I am dedicating this book to my mother Lillie P. Moncrief. After I lost my mom, I was inspired by God and my mom to write this book. My mom always felt like she didn't do enough or make a big difference in the world. This book shows that to be unfounded. I wish that she was here to see and read this book that has been inspired by her and God but somehow, I feel she can. My mom changed my life forever and her love for God was immense and wonderful to see! Mom this is for you and I want you to know that you did make a difference and made me a better man. I hope this book will touch the hearts of everyone who will read it because my mom was truly amazing and an angel on Earth!

Chapter 1

*

GOD

Who is God? We ask ourselves that every single day. I'm sure that if you ask anyone, they would all give you a different answer. Some will have amazing things to say about him and others not so nice things and others don't believe in him at all. In my whole thirty-five years of life all I can say is what I believe to be true and that's God is nothing less than amazing.

I can go into what the bible say he is the beginning and the end, omnipresent, Alpha and Omega and more. We know all those things to be true, but I can give my take on who God is to me. God has been a healer, miracle worker and inspiration in my life. There were times when

I stopped believing or even questioned his existence, but I know one thing to be true that there is a God!

I learned in life that if you quiet yourself and listen you will hear him. There is a little voice that will lead you and guide you. I also learned that all he wants is for us to not only listen to him but also talk to him. God is everywhere at every moment, 24/7, 365 days a year. Even when I felt like he wasn't with me he was guiding and leading me. There were times I felt alone especially when there was no one around to talk too but God was there every single time.

Then the day came when my mom became sick which I will go into much more detail in the next chapter, but he healed her. There was a time when I myself became sick and he healed me. I will go into more detail about my mom and me in the next few chapters, but I hope that I have your attention so far. God has been the most constant and consistent being in my life.

I find comfort in knowing that God loves me more than anyone and that he only wants the best for you and me. I think of God like an earthly parent he can see when something is wrong and only wants to see us happy. He knows when we are not being truthful and will love us and help us even when we caused all the chaos and trouble. I believe that just like an earthly parent he can see through our friends and know who is good for us and who is not. Believe it or not God has a love for us not even our parents have.

We may not agree with his decisions for us, but you best believe that he knows best and can see things that we cannot see. There were a lot of situations in my life when I felt like I knew what's best and I was proved wrong. So many times, I wanted what I wanted and felt like I was denied but a denial is not a no. Many times, God has something so much better than what we could ever dream possible. I have learned patience in my relationship with God. I have always been the spoiled I want it and need it NOW! But God was always there saying no you don't need it now you just want it. I learned that with patience and God any and everything is possible!

James 1:17(NIV) says "Every good and perfect gift is from above, coming down from the Father of the heavenly lights, who does not change like shifting shadows." This scripture really sticks with me because all our blessings come from God and shows that he will never change not today, not tomorrow, NEVER! One thing I have learned is to always give God praise for everything good and bad. I know you are probably saying "Wait a minute even for the bad stuff?" My answer is yes because everything we go through is to make us stronger. Just because we believe in God doesn't mean that bad things won't happen, but what it guarantees is that he will guide us through the storm and that he will never leave us or forsake us!

Matthew 6:26(NIV) says "Look at the birds of the air, they do not sow or reap, or store away in barns, and yet your heavenly Father feeds them. Are you not much more valuable than they?" This is another scripture that speaks to me. Think about it the birds fly around freely not sowing or planting seeds, yet they still are taken care of. God is so amazing that he takes care of us and we don't even realize it at times. I think of God as a 24/7 guard, counselor, and provider. Its up to us to realize that and take advantage of his never changing hand.

2 Corinthians 6:18(NIV) "I will be a Father to you, and you will be my sons and daughters, says the Lord Almighty." God created all of us to have a relationship not only with each other as friends, marriage, family, society and the church but with him as well. Our relationship with God is by far the most important relationship that we can have. I believe when our relationship with God is on track then all our other relationships will fall into place, and the toxic ones will find their way out.

God is so amazing that he wants nothing but the best for us and that includes the people in our lives. I know for me I tried to hold onto some people that God was trying to remove from my life. I have come to realize that some people are only meant to be in our lives for a season. We try to salvage a toxic relationship and sometimes end up blocking our own blessings. I have learned to let God take the lead because he knows best and only wants the best for you and me!

God never fails to amaze me! He wants us to be the best and have the best! His plans for us is not our own and sometimes it's hard to see the bigger picture. Even when we don't follow his plans or rebel, he is still there waiting for us ready to forgive and love us. It's hard for us to forgive something especially when it hurts. God is not like that he dislikes the sin or disobedience, but he is always there ready for us to learn from it and forgive us. We shouldn't just continue to disobey him knowing he will forgive us. We should want to do and be better, strive to be more God-like I mean why not we are made in his image.

Imagine that being made in his image do you realize how much power we possess? Never feel like God doesn't understand because he truly does. He knows all and sees all, he knows our pain, hurt, cares, worries and our happiness. Always remember that wc are made in his image and I believe that there is so much power in that alone! The bible says that (Proverbs 18:21 NIV) "The tongue has the power of life and death, and those who love it will eat it's fruit." When God created everything, he just spoke it and it was so. Remember to be very careful what you speak into your life because there is so much power in the words that we speak.

"When God spoke let there be light there was light. We are made in his image, so whenever we speak it can be good or bad, it can either hurt or it can make us feel good. Sometimes words can be encouraging, and sometime words can discourage. So, we all must watch and be careful how we speak to each other. We can say something hurtful to someone and that person will walk away with the pain forever or we can say something nice and put a smile on a person face. They will walk away with a cheerful heart. So, let us try to build each other up with confidence and to inspire each other to give strength and courage to do things. That will make it more enjoyable for them. Let us love one another, encourage each other. So, we will all have a smile on our face." -Mom

No matter if you believe in God or not it wouldn't hurt to find out more about him because honestly, he knows everything about us. He knows us better than we know ourselves, he knows every need, every want, every care that we have but he also knows what is best for us. I cannot say this enough that just because we believe in him does not mean that life will always be good. One thing I can guarantee is that God will be there to see you through the good and the bad. He is our foundation when our lives are having an earthquake. He is our shelter when our life is going through a hurricane. Always remember that God will never leave us NEVER!

Chapter 2

✳

MY MOM

"This pain does not belong to me, this is God pain. So, I am going to give it to him. Take the weight off yourself and give it to God! Jesus will sustain you."

The words above are from my beautiful, amazing, caring, giving, funny, God filled mother Lillie P. Moncrief. This chapter will be all about my mother, I could write a whole book about her and maybe one day I will. My mom was born on January 20th, 1953 to Joe and Mandy Moncrief. My mom grew up in Montrose, Mississippi a very small town. She was one of many children and loved by everyone.

I refer to my mom as Queen, my twin, best friend, my sister so if you hear any of these words then you will know that I am referring to my mother. My queen was my everything she loved me unconditionally with all of her being and heart. She molded me into the man that I am today, my twin instilled in me things that I will forever hold onto. My mom is the reason that I believe in God and want a closer relationship with him.

Now my mom was not only a daughter, sister, aunt, mother and more she was a singer, beautician, the life of any event and all-around beauty! I remember being called my mom shadow because I was always up under her and followed her wherever she went. She was my hero and I was hers, she would always say that I was "The wind beneath her wings." And honestly, she was mine as well. She raised my brother and I the best way she knew how being a single mother. I always believed that my mom went above and beyond for my brother and I. Believe me when I say that my mother was the best mother to ever walk this Earth! I was so blessed to have her as my mother, she would give the shirt off her back for my brother and me.

My best friend had a laugh and smile that was so infectious, I'm smiling just thinking about her. She knew when something was wrong even when I felt like everything was right. It was like my mom could see in the future, now I realize that it was the gift of discernment. No matter where I was in the world she could feel, dream and see things. I would get annoyed sometime because she knew everything and the more I denied the more she would push until I confess.

No one could ever deny the effect that my mom had on everyone that she encountered. She had such a sweet and nurturing spirit. She could do no wrong in my eyes and she was my protector and I was hers. Although she was human, she was my super hero, she would always swoop in and save the day! I felt like she had powers and strength that I wish I had. Not to mention she was one of the best cooks I have ever met in my life!

As I mentioned earlier, she is the reason that I started going to church and believing in God. I remember a church opened next door to our house called True Vine Fellowship Ministries and she said as plain as day "We are going to church". There wasn't any room for NO with my mom because she wanted my brother and I to know God! She grew up in the church and she wanted us to have that opportunity to fellowship, worship and grow. This is when my relationship with God took off and made me the man that I am today. I can say this a million times that my mom is the reason that I have such a strong belief and relationship with God.

You would think that my mom lived a pain free and always happy life, but she didn't. She would always drive me to my high school and pick me up. During the year

2000 when I was 16, she began having trouble seeing and experiencing severe headaches. Although she had trouble seeing she still would drive me to school. Until one day I remember being called to the hospital and she told my brother and I the devastating news that she had been diagnosed with a brain tumor. I cried and cried because I felt like my mom, my best friend, my twin, my super hero was slipping away from me. Then I was told that it was non-malignant thank God and that she would have to have surgery. I think the surgery scared me more than hearing the news that she had a brain tumor.

My mom told me that when she heard the news that she ran out of the hospital room. I know how hard it was for her to hear such news. I also know that one of the first things that came to her mind was my brother and I. She was always concerned about us day and night and I'm sure she worried about who would take care of us and my stepdad. I don't think there is any type of preparation you can do to ready yourself for such a big surgery as brain surgery. The day came when she had the surgery at one of the best hospitals in the tri-state area Mount Sinai in NYC.

She wasn't supposed to have the surgery there but thanks to God her doctor requested Mount Sinai because it was the best place to have a surgery such as this.

The surgery was successful, and I could rest my mind for only a second because I was not prepared to see my mom post-surgery and when I did, she had all these tubes hooked up to her and her head was wrapped in so many bandages. I remember crying because this is my mom, my everything and again I felt as if she was slipping away. I prayed and prayed, the church we were members of continued to pray as well.

Then the day came when I was in church for Sunday service and was called out by my dad because the doctors had informed him that my mom condition had changed from stable to worst. We rushed to NYC and she had a stroke and pneumonia as well. I remember holding her hand and just sobbing. She opened her eyes and although a tube was down her throat, she fixed her mouth to say, "What's wrong?". I just fixed my face best I can because I didn't want her worrying about my tears. My mom after all she been through was still concerned about me.

I remember praying to God asking him to let my mom live to see me graduate from high school. At that time, I didn't realize that when I ask God for something to not put him in a box because he can do any and everything. All I could think about was my mom seeing me graduate that's any parents dream to see their child graduate from high school and college. God brought my mom through and she was released from Mount Sinai and sent to another hospital in New Jersey closer to home for her recovery. I visited my mom almost everyday and I remember catching a cold and when she found out she was begging everyone to release her because she had to get home to take care of me. That was my mom always thinking of someone especially her children before herself.

Her rehabilitation took a couple of months, but she was finally released and sent home. I remember being overjoyed but at the same time nervous because it was such a delicate time. I was there for my mom waiting on her every need. I wanted to make sure that she didn't have to do too much until she was 100% again. A couple of months went by and the opportunity came for me to go to Disney World with the church and my mom being the amazing woman that she was made sure I was able to go at the last minute. My mom was always like that wanting to make sure I was happy and ok. She told me that I deserved to go because of everything that went on with her and how stressful it was.

Then June 2001 came around and guess who came to my graduation? My mother! She came in there with her beautiful hair that she was so afraid of losing when she found out about her brain tumor. You could not tell that my mom had hip replacements nor brain surgery. Yes, my mom had hip replacements as well. She was so beautiful, and it was a very emotional moment for me because I was praying for this moment for so long. My queen was able to see her baby son graduate and she was so very proud!

I bet you are wondering wow your mom had total hip replacements and brain surgery all by the young age of 47 but she remained so beautiful and vibrant and most of all God-filled. She never gave up and later told me that seeing me in the hospital when I came to visit her gave her strength to want to go on and push through. She said that my brother and I are the main reason she wanted to live and fight. My mom was a walking miracle because doctors didn't think she would make it, but she survived and made it through! Glory be to God!

"Your adversity is an opportunity to grow. Thank God for his comfort and care for his children. Burnt but not bitter." – Mom

"If God could close the lion's mouth for Daniel, part the red sea for Moses, make the sun stand still for Joshua, open the prison for Peter, put a baby in Sarah arms, and raised Lazarus from the dead, then he can certainly take care of you! Have faith in him he won't let you down." – Mom

"God purpose for Paul is the same purpose he has for you and me, to know his son and become like him." Romans 8:29

"If its big enough to worry about, its big enough to pray about! You are an overcomer; your life is not over until God says its over." – Mom

Those excerpts were taken from my mom notebook one of three that I am adding to this very book. My mom wrote so many things in her notebooks and had conversations with God that I never knew about. I would always see her writing but thought she was writing things down from her favorite channels QVC or HSN but she also loved TBN so there are so many different things that I will cherish forever in her notebooks.

My mom faith in God was just amazing to watch. She was diagnosed with necrosis, lupus and had the brain tumor but it never kept her from praising God. When you have a praying mother there is nothing like it. Her prayers have kept me safe even during danger. I had God, Jesus the holy spirit, and my mom on my side and my mom reminded me everyday of the goodness of God. No matter how much she struggled, no matter how much pain she was in she still praised God. She knew that God would always take care of her despite whatever was going on.

"Heavenly father walk through my home and take away all my worries and any illness. Please watch over and heal my family and friends with peace, love and joy amen." – Mom

"Thank you, God, for keeping me safe through the night, and every time you wake me up to see another day. I thank God amen!" – Mom

"God is good, he is with me, he is for me. He is my provider, he is my healer, and he loves me, and I love him. Don't let your doubt be your dead end." – Mom

"Lord you carry me through all my storms, when I'm down you lift me up, when I'm weak you make me strong, when I have nothing you are my everything. Your grace is sufficient for me, thank you Lord!" – Mom

I learned so much from my mom not only about God but about myself and my inner strength. My mom showed me that I am stronger than I think, she also continued to show me that life isn't easy but with God I would make it through. She was a living, walking testimony and when she spoke her voice was so soft and angelic and to me, she could probably calm a lion with her voice. I have never met someone so giving and she would always ask if I needed any money although she was disabled, and her disability checks weren't much. Her thought was if my children are ok then I'm ok and if they are not ok then I'm not.

Whatever my mom went through in life she went through it with God on her mind and in her heart. No matter good or bad my mom involved God in everything, and not only have I been a witness to it, but I see it in the notebooks I refer to constantly in this book. I want you to see my mom and how she talked to God and I find it to be very inspiring and motivating. I aspire to be like my mom and to have conversations with God throughout my day like my mom.

"You are the God that heals me, you sent your word and heal my diseases. Father I put your name on my tongue, my brain, heart, my lungs, kidneys, my legs. Father I put your name on my whole body and father whatever I must go through today and everyday I go through with your strength. Today I can make it, through God who strengthens me." – Mom

As you can see my mother prayers were very powerful and I can use them in my everyday life. I feel as if my mom left me a blueprint to help me get through this thing called life. I'm still amazed reading all her words, thoughts and feelings. I know that because of her that I can make it through anything because I have God!

"God here I am, I know because you live inside my spirit. I give myself to you, guide me and teach me. Tell me what to say when I speak, teach me to be quiet when need be. I ask you father God to come in my body, every inch of my being. I love you father God have mercy on me, and the country we live. I give you praise in Jesus name that wherever I go Jesus is there standing with me to guide me in the right direction. On every plane, car, train and bus protect me and cover me in your blood, the blood of Jesus. Father I give you all the glory and praise and thank you for your grace and mercy. In Jesus name nothing but the name of Jesus, into your hands I give it all to you." – Mom

Not only did my mom pray for herself, family, and friends she prayed for the country and world leaders. She taught me that we must pray for everyone. As you can see in the prayer above, she asked God to have mercy on the country that we live in. I always thought to just pray for close friends and family but not everyone. I learned that everyone needs our prayers especially our world leaders. My mom taught me that you never know what someone is going through so why not just pray for them.

There was one time when I was sick, and no one knew what to do not even doctors, but my mom prayed and laid on me and somehow the next day I was better. I asked her what she did, and she said she prayed, and the holy spirit told her to lay on me. It was like she took the sickness away from me and put it somewhere else. There was a time that a little toddler was choking on something in church and my mom saved him by doing the Heimlich maneuver. There was also a time that I was choking on food and she was there to save the day. You see why I call her my super hero! My mom always knew what to do and always raised to the occasion no matter if it was physically or spiritually, she was there.

Unfortunately, my queen, my best friend, my super hero departed this world on her birthday January 20th, 2019. I remember her being in so much pain right before her death due to her lupus and she went into cardiac arrest in the ambulance. My mom was tired, and her heart couldn't take anymore, and I believe in my heart she was ready. She would always mention how much she missed her parents and sisters who passed before her. I cannot express how devastated I am because she was and is still my everything. I thank God that I had a moment to spend time with her on Christmas Day 2018 and she went all out and cooked me such a big meal that put such a big smile on my face. I remember telling her how thankful I was for her and the meal. She was so happy that day and we were happy to see each other. I spoke to her for the last time on the day she passed, and I told her I loved her and that I would see her tomorrow and she replied "I love you baby." Not knowing that would be the last time speaking to her.

Amazing I asked God to let my mom live to see me graduate from high school and that was in 2000 and I graduated in 2001. God exceeded my expectations and gave me nineteen more years with my mother. Although I cry a lot and I miss her with all my soul I find peace in knowing that no longer must she suffer, cry, or worry about me and my brother. I realize that a mother will always think about her children and their safety. A mother will want nothing but the best for her children and a mother will give her last for her children. My mother raised me in the way that I should go and that is with God may I never depart from that path!

I thank God for giving me such an angel on Earth. I thank God for everything I went through with my mom because that only made our relationship that much stronger. I thank God for giving my mom the wisdom and know how to raise my brother and me. I thank God for giving her the strength to persevere, encourage and pray for others. My mom taught me everything from always putting God first to cooking, praying, listening, loving and most of all never giving up! Mom you will forever be in my heart, mind, spirit and most of all my life! I will love you forever and our bond is unbreakable!

Chapter 3

———— �֍ ————

ME

Here I am writing a book about God, my mom and me. Never have I ever thought about writing a book like this but God and somehow, I feel like my mom put it in my heart. After the passing of my mom I had to get into a different mindset because I had to make all the arrangements and make sure that my mom had an amazing homegoing. Now that she is laid to rest in our home state of Mississippi, I'm starting to feel everything. Now that the adrenaline is gone, I'm left with my feelings, I'm left with the hurt, and the pain.

Then I hear my mom saying everything is going to be ok and just follow the path that she directed me too. My mom always wanted me to grow with God and continue to grow in him. We would talk about death and sometimes I would say mom I don't want to talk about it, and she would say "Why baby we all have to do it one day." I believe that every parent wants to know that their child will be ok if something were to happen to them.

Now I can be selfish and say why me, but I am not the only one who has experienced a mother passing. Even my mom lost her mother in 1992 and she died in my mothers' arms. So, I know that if my mom could make it through that, then I surely can make it through this with God help. I keep telling myself that and I find myself getting stronger and stronger.

I do have my moments because I am only human and, in those moments, especially the moments after I found out about my mom passing, I was angry. I was angry at God the most, why didn't he keep her here longer to see my special moments. I was angry at the EMT's, the hospital staff did they do enough to bring her back. I was even angry at myself, why wasn't I there. Then I realized that God's timing is not my own and that he kept her around for 19 more years after her brain surgery. I also had to realize that she was around for my special moments my high school prom/graduation, when I moved to Atlanta, bought my first house and graduated from college. Even if she couldn't be there in person for all of it, she knew of every special moment.

I couldn't blame the EMT's or the hospital staff because I know that they did everything they could have done and probably more. I also couldn't blame myself because her passing was so unexpected and for some reason, I have a feeling she wouldn't want me around to witness such a tragic moment like she did with her mother. I couldn't blame anyone because it was her time. My mother could've lived to be 100 years old and that still would not have been the right time. Death never happens at the right time and no matter how long a loved one is around it hurts, nonetheless.

I keep wanting to see her again like in a vision or a dream. I know that she is in a better place and resting but that doesn't stop me from wanting to see her or feel her presence. Then I find myself feeling her presence or even hearing her voice when I quiet myself down and relax my mind. My mom is with me and I realize that I have the best guardian angel anyone could ever have. I also know that I will see her again when it is my time. All I can do now is live for her, God and myself. I must continue and make a difference in this world.

I must share a story that most don't know about. In 2016 I became ill and I didn't know what was wrong with me. Doctors found out what was wrong and diagnosed me with gastroparesis. It is a condition that stops your stomach from working properly. Everything that I ate would not stay down. I couldn't even drink water without vomiting. I was in and out of the hospital and the doctors ran so many tests on me. They thought I had diabetes, cancer even thought I was bulimic because I was vomiting so much. Every test came back normal and I remained in the hospital, but I remember my mom bought a suitcase to come down to Atlanta.

At that time, I was a patient in the hospital and my mom said she wanted to stay in the hospital with me day and night. I had to beg her not to come because she was not 100% herself and I didn't want her uncomfortable in the hospital chairs or beds. I knew the stress of seeing me in the hospital wouldn't be good on her body or her mind. I was thankful when I convinced her to stay in New Jersey which took a lot of stress off me. Although deep down inside I did want her there because all I wanted to do was see and be around her. After all the test from a bone marrow biopsy, to inserting a feeding tube so that I can get some nutrients in me I was finally released.

I remember telling one of my best friends that I wanted to drive up to New Jersey to see my mom. I felt like she and God was the only ones who could heal me. My mom had these healing hands that only God can give someone. Although I was very weak and lost 50 pounds, I got up the strength and nerve to make the 13-hour drive. My friend didn't want me to go but I said I have to see my mom. I left the next day after being released out of the hospital with God and Ensure in my car. My mom was on the phone with me non-stop because she was so worried. I never told her during my drive how bad my leg was shaking because I was that weak.

Finally, I made it to New Jersey and as I parked my car, I could see my mom waiting for me at the door. She lived on the 3rd floor and I remember having trouble going up the steps because again my body was deprived of nutrients. I could barely make it up the stairs because while I was in the hospital, I stopped getting up to walk because I lost all hope. So here I am at my mom house and trying my best to make it up the stairs. Then I felt her hand on my back and her saying "You can do it, I'm right behind you". Before I knew it, I was at my mom door and she opened it.

I sat down in the living room so tired and drained. My mom stood there and hugged me so tight. From her helping me on the steps to the hug I felt a burden being lifted off me. I knew I made the right decision; do you know after months of not eating and vomiting that my mom cooked for me. I told her I was afraid of eating but she told me "You will not vomit". I remember eating and not vomiting, that was the first time in months that I held my food down.

Would you believe that I only vomited one time while being at my mom house and when I did, I remember being on the bathroom floor crying. My mom came to the bathroom door and told me "Get up, its not over, get up right now". At that very moment I felt strength and I got up. My mom and God did something the doctors couldn't, they healed me. My mom told me that one thing she never stopped doing was praying. She called all her favorite prayer lines and even gave my name so that they could pray for me.

I remember not being able to sleep most nights so I would usually toss and turn all night or walk back and forth through the house. Usually whenever I went pass my mom room she would instantly wake up. It's like she felt my presence because when I walk, I'm always in stealth mode, no one can hear me. But my mom would wake up and ask what was wrong. She would tell me to get in the bed with her and although she was tired, she would talk to me until I fell asleep. Most of the time just being next to her would help me relax and I would fall asleep.

I never seen my mom cry in front of me although I knew she did because it was so hard on her. My angel, my queen, my twin helped heal me. She would even help clean my feeding tube. My eyes are tearing up as I type this because my mom did that for me. God did that for me. After a couple months I was ready to go back to

Atlanta and I never vomited again. I always thanked my mom and she would always say "Don't thank me just give praise to God'. She would always say it was him and not her and that God was only working through her.

Now you see why I said in the previous chapter that my mom was my everything my superhero. She was around when I got bullied in school and always told me to hold my head up high. Now I'm sitting here like who can I turn to when I need help, when I need to talk. Then it hit me the one I should turn too is the one my mom always spoke of and that one is God. My mom leaned on him so much and I now realize that is what I must do as well. I am not alone, and I do have someone to talk to my heavenly father God. I am not doing none of this on my own because he is with me.

God has put so many great and amazing people in my life and I have them to talk to as well or spend time with. I want to continue to make my mom proud and know that none of the things she taught me were in vain. I want her to know that I was listening, watching and taking everything in. I can and I will spread her message of love, prayer and understanding. I have her and God strength within me and I will never forget that.

"I can do all things through Christ who strengthens me." Philippians 4:13

"Even though I walk through the darkest valley, I will fear no evil, for you are with me; your rod and your stuff, they comfort me." Psalm 23:4

It's amazing that some of the scriptures that are in this book are some of the same scriptures that my mom taught me. These scriptures were also inspired by God, so I feel as if I have the blueprint laid out before me from God and my mom as well. I find it hard at times to devote time to reading the bible and spending time with God but growing up I've watched my mom do it and it was so inspiring to watch. I could see how her relationship with God and reading the holy word had changed her.

I realize that I must work on my relationship with God just as I work on my earthly relationships. A relationship cannot grow if you don't put in the work to learn more about the person or being you are in a relationship with. There are times when I'm doing nothing and those are the times that I can dedicate to praying or reading the word. I also come to find that I can also dedicate time to God even in my busy moments. I started talking to him even while at work or when I'm out at a party. I believe that God wants what's best for us so why not spend the time to get to know him and love him just as he loves us. I don't understand everything that has happened in my life, but I always rely on this scripture.

"Trust in the Lord with all your heart; do not depend on your own understanding. Seek his will in all you do, and he will show you which path to take." Proverbs 3: 5-6 (NLT)

When I read that scripture, it proves to me that my heavenly father knows best and again only wants what's best for me. God can see things that we cannot see, and he knows things that we do not know. When I'm running late sometimes it is God keeping me from harm or when I don't get that job I wanted it's because he has something better. I must lean on his understanding because if I lean on my own, I would never get anywhere and would probably be very upset for most of my life.

God you are my everything and you were everything to my mother! I want to thank you for everything that I have and everything that will come. I now know that no matter what happens in my life that you will be there with me. I know that you will be there to guide me and love me. I just want to thank you for everything and most of all I want to thank you for my mother she was the greatest gift you could give me. I cannot say that enough because my mother was truly my angel on Earth and my best friend. Thank you mom and I will forever love you and I hope that I am making you proud as you look down on me. Thank you heavenly father! – O-haji

Chapter 4

* * *

MY MOTHERS' WORDS

Here you will find words from my mothers' notebook. I hope that her words can encourage you in some way. I hope that her words can help you in your own conversations with God. I know for me sometimes I don't know what to say but reading her words help me and inspire me. Also, my mom taught me something else that when I don't know what to say then just say "Jesus". God understands what we are trying to say even when we don't know what to say. Mom this is in honor of you and I hope that you are smiling.

Father God protect me from all the evil of the world today and every day. – Mom

It does not matter what is going on in the world today, what matters is the word of God in us. – Mom

We are not here to see who we can put down. We are here to build each other up. – Mom

We are not in control over anything. God is in control sometime in life we must be brought down, before we are built up. – Mom

God works through you and I. He equips us with what we need. We must ask him and listen to hear him and be patient. – Mom

Father whenever I ask for something and it is not for me, are it's the wrong time to have what I ask for help me to find peace in it. Father I trust you to give me what I need. – Mom

Debt sometime can make a person sick. It is easier to get in debt than it is to get out. We always think about feeling good now, so we buy things and get in debt but what about tomorrow. It is easier to get in trouble than it is to get out. Being greedy can get you in trouble, Father God you give us what we need but we always want more. – Mom

God in the name of Jesus these chains of pain will be broken, chain of hurt, no peace, chain of poverty shall be broken now in the name of Jesus. I have faith in his name, the name of Jesus. I will not lay down and die I will fight in the name of Jesus. I pray that my health be restored in

Jesus name. Anything in my life that is not of you remove it in Jesus name. – Mom

Heavenly father thank you for giving me a way to talk to you as I read the bible today. Please send your holy spirit to meet with me and speak to me through your word amen.

Father show me the best path for my life. God may respond to you through the holy spirit or he may reveal wisdom to you through his word. As you draw closer to God, you'll begin to feel love and the compassion he has for all his people growing inside of you. You will start looking for ways to connect with people to share with them everything God has given you, so that they may become closer to God and want to get to know him through his word. - Mom

Author Page

*

I'm O-haji Moncrief born on September 17th, 1983 in Laurel, Mississippi. I spent a few years in Mississippi but was raised in Paterson, NJ by my amazing mother and Dallas my dad. I attended Rosa L. Parks Arts High School a performing arts high school in Paterson where my major was drama.

I have always had a passion for the arts especially drama and writing. This is my first book and I intend to write more.

Printed in the United States
By Bookmasters